28 Ways To Love You

By: Amalia B. Gratteri

First Printing, 2016
ISBN: 978-0-9971817-8-4

To those who are always looking for new ways to
redefine their love.

#1

I promise to love myself so that I
don't forget how to love you.
Wholly and unconditionally.

♥

#2

I hear you. Not just your words, but the feeling behind them. I will listen in order to know your heart. And I will listen until I understand.

♥

#3

Random kisses and gentle touches. You will never have to doubt my attraction to you that goes as deep as your soul right to the surface of your skin.

♥

#4

I will follow you with my trust, and lead when I must. My support will never waiver as we learn this life together.

♥

#5

Sweet nothings always mean something. I will remember the little things, because they make up the big things.

♥

#6

Sometimes a simple "I love you"
will suffice.

♥

#7

Let me undress your worries.
Let down your guard with me,
and I'll take care of you.

♥

#8

Let me nurture your body with a home cooked meal. Good food isn't just the way to your heart, it's experiencing new tastes together so that we can satisfy each other's cravings.

♥

#9

Eyes filled with longing and admiration. That one look says it all. That one look conveys my love for you all in one glance.

♥

#10

Nothing says love like support through the ups and downs. No matter what life throws at us, I got you.

♥

#11

Love isn't all roses. So I will
remember the words "I'm
sorry," and "I forgive you."
Because I love you enough to let
go of my pride.

❤

#12

Your love inspires me to be a better version of myself. Loving you is knowing how to love myself.

♥

#13

Love is knowing when to put you first. I know now that it isn't always just about what I want, but what's best for us.

♥

#14

Loving you is not needing a special day to show you because every day is a celebration of our love.

♥

#15

My fingers intertwined into
yours - holding hands shows you
I need you, and I want you with
the power of touch.

♥

#16

I wrote a list of your favorite
things. Knowing what brings you
joy, brings me joy. And brings me
closer to loving the parts of your
heart that only few know.

♥

#17

Sharing moments or things that make me think of you when we are away from each other is a reminder you're always in my thoughts, even when you aren't next to me.

♥

#18

I want you to know that I believe in you. Even when your back is against the wall and it feels the world is against you. I'll always be for you.

❤

#19

I promise to always be honest
with you because loving you
means giving nothing less than
what you deserve - the truth.

♥

#20

Loving you means giving you the
space to grow into who you were
meant to become.

♥

#21

I will spill my passion into you.
My words, the match. Your lips,
the fire. And you, the oxygen
that keeps me going.

♥

#22

I will write novels with my
tongue.

❤

#23

I promise to give you my full, undivided attention. No distractions, just you and me.

♥

#24

Loving you is learning you. I will never stop getting to know who you are and the person you are becoming.

♥

#25

Love is patient. I will get
frustrated and I will get mad, but
I'll always return to love.

♥

#26

If I forgot to tell you today - I appreciate you.

♥

#27

Hugs and plenty of them. I will embrace you mentally, emotionally, and spiritually. But most of all, physically.

♥

#28

I will never forget why I fell in love with you. And I will find ways to remind you every day for the rest of my life.

♥

Contact:

Email: abgratteri@hotmail.com
Facebook: www.facebook.com/AmaliaG.Poetry
Twitter: SpeakLoveLife
Instagram: SpeakLifeLove